UNITED STATES BY REGION

*People and Places of the*
# MIDWEST
By Kassandra Radomski

Consultant:
Dr. David Lanegran
John S. Holl Professor of Geography
Macalester College
St. Paul, Minnesota

**CAPSTONE PRESS**
a capstone imprint

Fact Finders Books are published by Capstone Press,
1710 Roe Crest Drive, North Mankato, Minnesota 56003
www.mycapstone.com

Copyright © 2017 by Capstone Press, a Capstone imprint. All rights reserved. No part of this publication may be reproduced in whole or in part, or stored in a retrieval system, or transmitted in any form or by any means, electronic, mechanical, photocopying, recording, or otherwise, without written permission of the publisher.

**Library of Congress Cataloging-in-Publication Data**
Names: Radomski, Kassandra.
Title: People and places of the Midwest / by Kassandra Radomski.
Description: North Mankato, Minnesota : Capstone Press, 2017. | Series: Fact finders. United States by region. | Audience: Grades 4 to 6.? | Includes bibliographical references and index.
Identifiers: LCCN 2016009135 | ISBN 9781515724407 (library binding) | ISBN 9781515724452 (paperback) | ISBN 9781515724506 (PDF)
Subjects: LCSH: Middle West—Juvenile literature. | Middle West—Geography—Juvenile literature. | Middle West—Description and travel—Juvenile literature. | Middle West—Social conditions—Juvenile literature.
Classification: LCC F351 .R33 2017 | DDC 977--dc23
LC record available at http://lccn.loc.gov/2016009135

**Editorial Credits**
Angie Kaelberer, editor; Cynthia Della-Rovere, designer; Svetlana Zhurkin, media researcher; Laura Manthe, production specialist

**Photo Credits**
Glow Images: ImageBROKER, cover (top); Library of Congress, 23, 29; Newscom: blickwinkel/picture alliance/U. Brunbauer, 17, ImageBROKER/Jim West, 22, Reuters/Eric Miller, 25; North Wind Picture Archives, 9; Shutterstock: Action Sports Photography, 27, Doug Lemke, cover (bottom), Elizabeth C. Zurek, 15, Everett Historical, 11, 13, July Flower, 18–19, Nagel Photography, 10, Steven Frame, 6, Tony Campbell, 21

Design and Map Elements by Shutterstock

# Table of Contents

Introduction . . . . . . . . . . . . . . . . . . . . . . . . .4

Chapter 1: History and Growth . . . . . . .8

Chapter 2: Land and Climate . . . . . . . .14

Chapter 3: Jobs and Economy . . . . . . .20

Chapter 4: People and Culture . . . . . . .24

*Glossary* . . . . . . . . . . . . . . . . . . . . . . . . . . . *30*

*Read More* . . . . . . . . . . . . . . . . . . . . . . . . . *31*

*Internet Sites* . . . . . . . . . . . . . . . . . . . . . . . *31*

*Index* . . . . . . . . . . . . . . . . . . . . . . . . . . . . . *32*

# Introduction

When you think of the Midwest, you might picture endless fields of wheat and corn. You may also think of cows grazing in green pastures. But this isn't a complete picture. When traveling in the Midwest, you'll also see tall skyscrapers in cities that include Chicago, Illinois; Minneapolis, Minnesota; and Kansas City, Missouri.

The Midwest includes the 12 states in the middle of the United States. They are Illinois, Indiana, Iowa, Kansas, Michigan, Minnesota, Missouri, Nebraska, North Dakota, Ohio, South Dakota, and Wisconsin.

Michigan, Minnesota, Kansas, Nebraska, North Dakota, and South Dakota rank in the top 20 states by area. But many midwestern states don't have large populations. Illinois has the most people. North Dakota has the fewest.

# The Midwest Region by Rank

Let's see how the states in the Midwest compare to each other. This chart includes each state in the Midwest and ranks it by population and area. Also included are each state's capital and nickname. Some of the nicknames are easy to understand, such as Michigan being the Great Lakes State. But how do you think Missouri became the Show-Me State?

In South Dakota tourists can visit Mount Rushmore National Memorial.

| State | Population | Rank | Square Miles | Rank | Capital | Nickname |
|---|---|---|---|---|---|---|
| Illinois | 12,880,580 | 5 | 57,918 | 25 | Springfield | Prairie State |
| Indiana | 6,596,855 | 16 | 36,420 | 38 | Indianapolis | Hoosier State |
| Iowa | 3,107,126 | 30 | 56,276 | 26 | Des Moines | Hawkeye State |
| Kansas | 2,904,021 | 34 | 82,282 | 15 | Topeka | Sunflower State |
| Michigan | 9,909,877 | 10 | 96,810 | 11 | Lansing | Great Lakes State |
| Minnesota | 5,547,173 | 21 | 86,943 | 12 | St. Paul | North Star State |
| Missouri | 6,063,589 | 18 | 69,709 | 21 | Jefferson City | Show-Me State |
| Nebraska | 1,881,503 | 37 | 77,358 | 16 | Lincoln | Cornhusker State |
| North Dakota | 739,482 | 47 | 70,704 | 19 | Bismarck | Peace Garden State |
| Ohio | 11,594,163 | 7 | 44,828 | 34 | Columbus | Buckeye State |
| South Dakota | 853,175 | 46 | 77,121 | 17 | Pierre | Mount Rushmore State |
| Wisconsin | 5,757,564 | 20 | 65,503 | 22 | Madison | Badger State |

## Chapter 1
# History and Growth

The Midwest is rich in geography and natural resources. American Indians, such as the Dakota, Ojibwe, and Menominee, lived there long before European explorers arrived. Many tribes moved around as they hunted huge buffalo herds on the Great **Plains**. Plains Indians used the buffalo for food, clothing, and shelter. Other tribes, such as the Ho-chunk, hunted for food but also raised crops.

Europeans knew the Indians were skilled hunters who could supply them with animal skins and furs. At first the two groups traded peacefully. As settlers arrived in the early 1800s, American Indians were pushed out of their lands.

> **plains:** a large, flat area of land with few trees

Plains Indians used the skins from wolves while they hunted buffalo. This helped keep them from sight.

# The Path to Statehood

After the United States won the Revolutionary War (1775–1783), the Northwest **Territory** came under American control. This area included what is now Illinois, Indiana, Michigan, Ohio, and Wisconsin. It also included part of Minnesota. Ohio was the first midwestern territory to become a state in 1803.

African-American people were made to work as slaves at the time. When Ohio, Illinois, and Indiana became states, they outlawed slavery.

> **territory:** an area of land under the control of a country

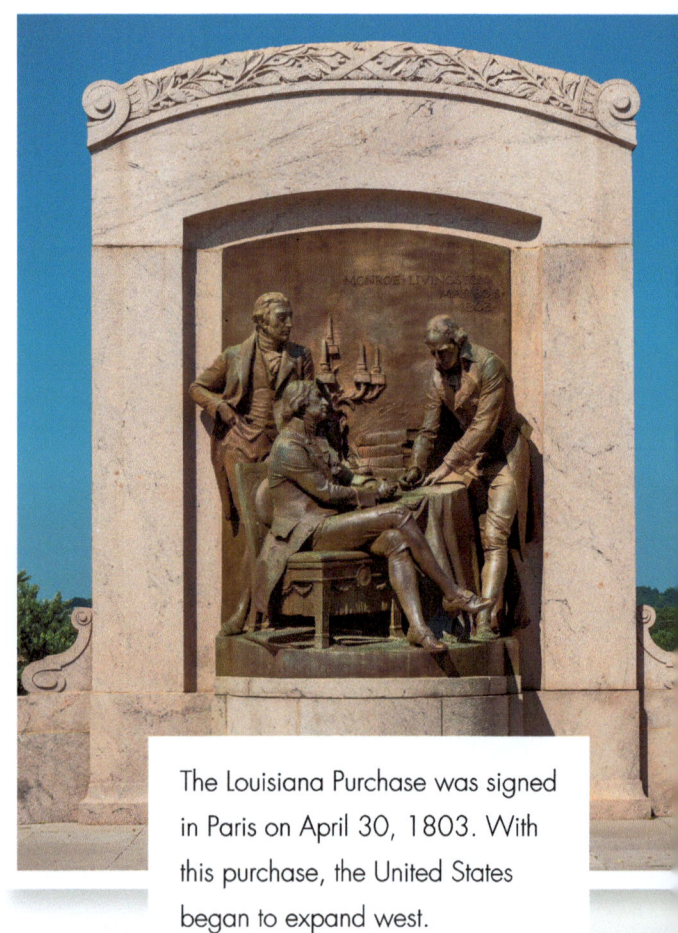

**FACT**

The tall Gateway Arch in St. Louis, Missouri, sits on the bank of the Mississippi River. It honors President Thomas Jefferson and his role in the Louisiana Purchase.

The Louisiana Purchase was signed in Paris on April 30, 1803. With this purchase, the United States began to expand west.

The other midwestern states were part of the huge Louisiana Territory. In 1803 President Thomas Jefferson bought a huge piece of land from France. This was the Louisiana Purchase. This 828,000 square-mile (2,144,510 square-kilometer) area included Iowa, Missouri, Kansas, and Nebraska. It also included large parts of Minnesota, North Dakota, and South Dakota.

With the Louisiana Purchase, the question of slavery became even more important. In 1820 the U.S. Congress passed the Missouri Compromise. This law allowed slavery in Missouri, but outlawed it in Maine.

**expedition:** a long journey made for a specific purpose

## Lewis and Clark Expedition

After the Louisiana Purchase, President Thomas Jefferson asked Meriwether Lewis and William Clark to explore the new land. On May 14, 1804, an **expedition** left St. Louis and set out on the Missouri River. They spent the winter of 1804–1805 at Fort Mandan in what is now North Dakota. There they met French trapper Toussaint Charbonneau. His wife, Sacajawea, was a Shoshone Indian. The couple joined the expedition. Sacajawea served as interpreter for the many Indian tribes they met along the way. The expedition reached the Pacific Ocean in November 1805. It returned to St. Louis in September 1806.

## Settlers Move to the Midwest

The slavery issue was one of the causes of the Civil War (1861–1865). After the Union won the war, slavery was outlawed in the entire country.

Much of the Midwest was still grassy **prairie** land. The U.S. government wanted people to build farms and towns. In 1862 the Homestead Act promised free land to anyone who lived on and farmed it for five years. People from eastern states and European **immigrants** took this offer.

As settlers moved to the Great Plains, they continued to push out American Indians. In 1874 gold was discovered in the Black Hills of South Dakota. This area was home to Lakota and Cheyenne people. The Indians battled the U.S. Army over the land. In 1876 the Indians had a major victory at the Battle of Little Bighorn in Montana. But the Indians were eventually forced to give up their land. They settled on small **reservations**.

**prairie:** a large area of flat or rolling grassland with few or no trees

**immigrant:** a person who moves from one country to live permanently in another

**reservation:** an area of land set aside by the U.S. government for American Indians

# The Dust Bowl

Farming in the Midwest was big business by the early 1920s. But poor farming practices and several years of **drought** caused land to dry up. Strong winds picked up the soil and turned the sky black with dirt. In the 1930s people started calling the area the Dust Bowl. Kansas and Nebraska were hit hard. About 2.5 million people in the Dust Bowl left to find work in such places as California. Things didn't improve until the rains returned and farmers learned better farming methods.

Dust storms were common in the Midwest during the 1930s. This one happened in Rolla, Kansas, on May 6, 1935.

**drought:** a long period of weather with little or no rainfall

## FACT

One of the worst dust storms of the 1930s hit the Great Plains on Sunday, April 14, 1935. The sky became pitch-black in the middle of the day. People called it "Black Sunday."

# Chapter 2

# Land and Climate

The Midwest has many lakes and rivers. Many cities were built near these water sources. The Midwest is also filled with plains and rolling hills.

## Great Plains Region

The Great Plains region includes all or part of 10 states. Four states are in the Midwest. These states are Kansas, Nebraska, North Dakota, and South Dakota.

The Great Plains gets its name because the area is flat, with few trees. Before Europeans arrived, tall grasses covered the plains states. It's a good area to grow crops. Rainfall amounts can vary, so crops must be able to grow in dry weather.

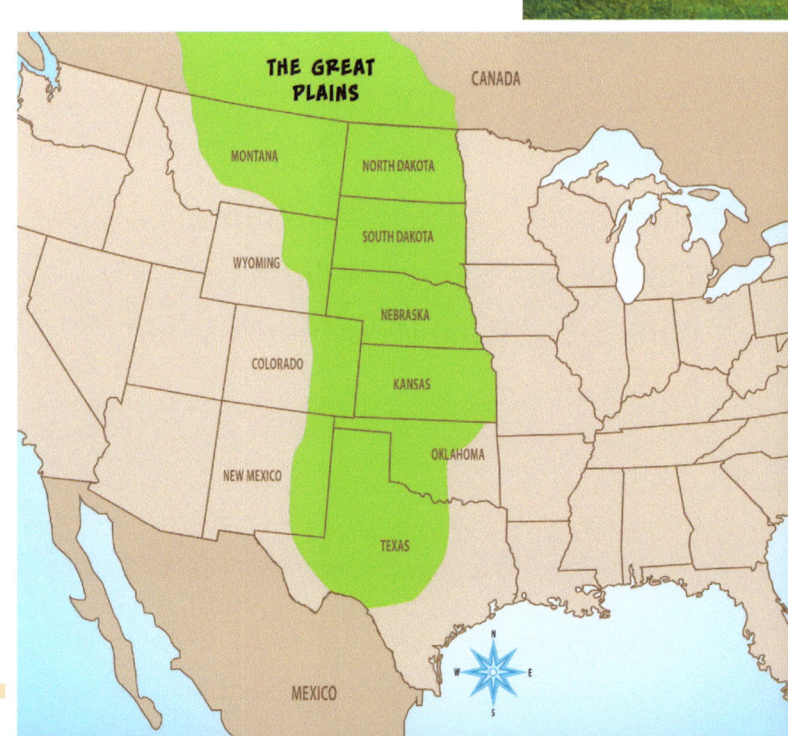

The plains in South Dakota are filled with grassy areas as far as the eye can see.

## Hills and Mountains

The Midwest is not all flat. Some places have hills and mountains. These areas include the Ozark Mountain Foothills in Missouri and the Black Hills in South Dakota.

The pine-covered Black Hills rise to more than 7,000 feet (2,133 meters). The mountains include the 5,725-foot (1,745-m) Mount Rushmore. Carved into the mountain are huge images of four U.S. Presidents. They are George Washington, Thomas Jefferson, Abraham Lincoln, and Theodore Roosevelt.

The Crazy Horse Memorial is another mountain carving in the Black Hills. It's planned to be even larger than Mount Rushmore. Crazy Horse was a Lakota warrior and chief who fought at the Battle of the Little Bighorn.

**FACT**

Korczak Ziolkowski began work on the Crazy Horse monument in 1948. He died in 1982 without completing the carving. His family continues his work. The monument's head was completed in 1998.

Crazy Horse Memorial can be found in the Black Hills in South Dakota. Once completed, the memorial will be the world's largest mountain carving.

# Lakes and Rivers

Four of the five Great Lakes touch parts of the Midwest. They are Lake Huron, Lake Superior, Lake Michigan, and Lake Erie. Lake Superior is the world's largest freshwater lake by surface area. The lake covers 31,800 square miles (82,362 square kilometers).

Minnesota is often called the "land of 10,000 lakes." Actually about 15,000 lakes of different sizes dot the state. People enjoy fishing, boating, and swimming in them.

The Ohio, Missouri, and Mississippi are major rivers in the region. They were the main Midwest transportation routes until the Civil War. After the war, railroads connected most of the country.

## Weather Extremes

Much of the Midwest has extreme differences in temperature. Winters can be cold and snowy, and summers are hot and humid. The coldest areas of the Midwest are northern North Dakota, Minnesota, Wisconsin, and Michigan. Kansas and Missouri have milder temperatures. Average winter high temperatures in northern Minnesota are about 20 degrees Fahrenheit (−7 degrees Celsius). In Missouri, a typical winter high temperature is around 45°F (7°C).

Cliffs can be found near Lake Superior in Minnesota.

**humid:** damp or moist

*Chapter 3*

# Jobs and Economy

The Midwest's riches include its many natural resources. These resources have helped create jobs. Important industries include farming, logging, mining, manufacturing, food processing, and printing.

## Farming and Ranching

With its rich soil, the Midwest is one of the world's top farming areas. All of the top 10 corn-producing states are in the Midwest. Iowa grows the most corn. North Dakota grows the most wheat, followed by Kansas. Soybeans, oats, sugar beets, and barley are other important crops.

Cattle are raised for dairy and beef. The second biggest dairy-producing state, after California, is Wisconsin. Minnesota and Michigan are also in the top 10.

Different types of crops are grown and harvested in the Midwest. This midwestern farmer is harvesting soybeans.

Other midwestern farms raise hogs. Iowa is the top pork-producing state. Illinois, Minnesota, Indiana, Missouri, Nebraska, Wisconsin, and Ohio also rank in the top 10.

Specialty crops are raised in the Midwest, too. Michigan produces more blueberries than any other state. Wisconsin grows lots of cranberries.

## FACT

The Great Plains region is sometimes called America's breadbasket. This is because its crops are used for making cereal and bread.

# Logging and Mining

Thick forests grow in Minnesota, Wisconsin, and Michigan. In the early 1800s, trees were used to build furniture and homes. Logs floated down nearby rivers to mills where they were cut into boards.

By the early 1900s, logs were used to make paper. Cities that grew with the logging industry include Wausau, Wisconsin, and Grand Rapids, Minnesota. Paper mills are still located in these areas.

The Midwest is also rich in minerals. Ships on the Great Lakes carry iron ore from mines in northern Minnesota and Michigan. They bring it to steel mills in Chicago, Detroit, Milwaukee, and Cleveland. But steel production isn't as important as it was in the past. In Chicago, many people work at large food and transportation companies. These include the airplane company Boeing. Companies in Milwaukee make tools and machinery.

Logs in Wisconsin are brought to a sawmill. A sawmill is a place where logs are cut into lumber.

Oil was discovered in western North Dakota in the 1950s. But it wasn't until the 2000s that technology allowed people to pump a large amount of oil from this area. In 2014 North Dakota wells were pumping more than one million barrels of oil per day. This is second only to Texas. But by 2015 oil prices had dropped. The boom slowed.

**FACT:** U.S. Steel Corporation founded the town of Gary, Indiana, in 1906. The steel mills provided jobs for most residents until the steel industry slowed in the 1960s.

## Henry Ford and Motor City

In the early 1900s, there were 125 auto companies in Detroit. Ford Motor Company was one of the most successful. In 1908 owner Henry Ford created the modern assembly line. This made production of cars go faster. Detroit became known as Motor City. Many African-Americans from the South moved there to work in the auto factories. Life in Detroit began to change in the 1950s and 1960s. During this time auto companies started moving production to other areas. The city lost thousands of manufacturing jobs, and many people left.

# Chapter 4

# People and Culture

The Midwest includes people from many backgrounds. People from Canada, New England, and the South settled in the Midwest. Many people also came from Europe.

## Settling the Midwest

Immigrants who moved to the United States often lived near others from the same country. Many German immigrants settled in Milwaukee, Wisconsin; St. Louis, Missouri; and Cincinnati, Ohio. People from Norway and Sweden lived in the Dakotas, Minnesota, Wisconsin, and Iowa. Staying close made it easier for them to keep their native language, customs, and religion. They also introduced new foods and music to the places they settled.

Midwestern industry took off in the late 1800s and early 1900s. People moved to big cities, such as Chicago, Detroit, Milwaukee, Minneapolis, and Cleveland. People also settled near iron ore mines in Minnesota and Michigan.

Immigration to the Midwest continued after World War II. People came from Europe, Asia, Latin America, and Africa. In the 1970s and 1980s, Hmong people from southeast Asia settled in Minnesota and Wisconsin. Minnesota is also the home of many people from Somalia, Africa.

These Somali girls are enjoying a game of basketball in a Minnesota park.

# Food and Festivals

The Midwest is known for its "comfort food," such as casseroles and mashed potatoes. But visitors enjoy other specialties as well. Kansas City is famous for its barbecue. Meat is slowly smoked over wood fires and covered in tangy sauce. People in Chicago feast on the city's deep-dish pizza.

County and state fairs are held each summer throughout the Midwest. At the fairs, people show off their baking, crafts, and farm animals. Fairs also feature carnivals, concerts, rodeos, and all kinds of food. Minnesota and Iowa host two of the biggest state fairs in the country. Both are famous for foods on a stick. They allow people to eat as they walk to fair attractions.

Each Memorial Day weekend, thousands of auto racing fans head to Indianapolis Motor Speedway in Indiana. Since 1911, the world's best racers have competed in the famous 500-mile (805-km) Indy 500.

The Indy 500 is a popular racing event in the Midwest. Drivers race around a track to win a trophy and prize money.

# Famous Midwesterners

Many midwesterners have done important things. Orville and Wilbur Wright lived in Dayton, Ohio. They are known for building and flying the first airplane in North Carolina in 1903. Pilot Amelia Earhart was from Kansas. In 1932 she became the first woman pilot to cross the Atlantic Ocean alone. Ohio native John Glenn was the first American to orbit Earth in 1962. In 1969 Ohio native Neil Armstrong became the first person to walk on the moon.

Several U.S. Presidents lived in the Midwest, too. Abraham Lincoln lived in Indiana and Illinois. Missouri native Harry Truman was a U.S. Senator before he became president in 1945. Dwight Eisenhower grew up in Abilene, Kansas. Herbert Hoover was born in Iowa, and Gerald Ford was from Michigan. Barack Obama lived in Chicago before becoming the 44th president.

Amelia Earhart was the first female pilot to fly across the Atlantic Ocean. She later disappeared in 1937.

The Midwest has a rich history and beautiful natural resources. It's filled with lively cities and friendly small towns. Both visitors and the people who call it home enjoy all it has to offer.

# Glossary

**drought** (DROUT)—a long period of weather with little or no rainfall

**expedition** (ek-spuh-DI-shuhn)—a long journey made for a specific purpose

**humid** (HYOO-mid)—damp or moist

**immigrant** (IM-uh-gruhnt)—a person who moves from one country to live permanently in another

**plains** (PLAYNZ)—a large, flat area of land with few trees

**prairie** (PRAIR-ee)—a large area of flat or rolling grassland with few or no trees

**reservation** (rez-er-VAY-shuhn)—an area of land set aside by the U.S. government for American Indians

**territory** (TER-uh-tor-ee)—an area of land under the control of a country

# Read More

**Allen, Nancy Kelly.** *Midwest and Great Lakes Regions.* United States Regions. Vero Beach, Fla.: Rourke Educational Media, 2015.

**Bartley, Niccole.** *The Midwest.* Land that I Love: Regions of the United States. New York: PowerKids Press, 2015.

**Connors, Kathleen.** *Let's Explore the Midwest.* Road Trip: Exploring America's Regions. New York: Gareth Stevens Publishing, 2014.

**Rau, Dana Meachen.** *The Midwest.* A True Book. New York: Children's Press, 2012.

# Internet Sites

FactHound offers a safe, fun way to find Internet sites related to this book. All of the sites on FactHound have been researched by our staff.

Here's all you do:

Visit www.facthound.com

Type in this code: 9781515724407

Check out projects, games and lots more at
www.capstonekids.com

# Index

American Indians, 8, 12
    Crazy Horse, 16
    Sacajawea, 11

animals, 8, 26

Black Hills, 12, 16

cities, 4, 14, 22, 23, 26, 29
    Chicago, 4, 22, 25, 26, 28
    Detroit, 22, 23,
    Indianapolis, 7, 27
    Kansas City, 4, 26
    Milwaukee, 22, 24, 25
    Minneapolis, 4, 25

Civil War, 12, 18,

Clark, William, 11

Dust Bowl, 13,

Earhart, Amelia, 28

farms, 12, 13, 20, 21

festivals, 26

food, 8, 20, 22, 24, 26

Ford, Henry, 23

forests, 22

Gateway Arch, 10

Great Plains, 8, 12, 13, 14, 21

Jefferson, Thomas, 10, 11, 16

jobs, 20, 23,

lakes, 6, 7, 14, 18, 22

land, 8, 12, 13, 14, 18
    prairies, 7, 12

Lewis, Meriwether, 11

Little Bighorn, Battle of, 12, 16

Louisiana Purchase, 10, 11

manufacturing, 20, 23,

mining, 20

Missouri Compromise, 11

oil, 23

presidents, U.S., 10, 11, 16, 28

rain, 13, 14

rivers, 14, 18, 22

Rushmore, Mount, 7, 16

slavery, 10, 11, 12,

temperatures, 19

Wright, Orville and Wilbur, 28